T0195559

—COLORED—
DIAMONDS

A book of poems and
valuable lessons learned

ROBYN HARRIS AND RUTH BANKS

authorHOUSE®

AuthorHouse™
1663 Liberty Drive
Bloomington, IN 47403
www.authorhouse.com
Phone: 1 (800) 839-8640

Published by AuthorHouse 02/29/2020

ISBN: 978-1-7283-4855-1 (sc)
ISBN: 978-1-7283-4854-4 (e)

Library of Congress Control Number: 2020903885

Print information available on the last page.

This book is printed on acid-free paper.

*In Loving Memory and Dedication of
Virginia Ellington, where it all began.*

THE DEEP BLUE SEA

The deep blue sea
Always stares at me
Cause when things go wrong
We will sing a song
But when things go right
We will see the light
Now will you tell me
Whether I'm wrong or right
And when that's all done
We will say goodnight

Robyn Harris
Poem written at the age of 6 years old

STRENGTH

The day had been swallowed
By darkness that fell
As I hit the streets walking
With fury entailed

I did not know where
Which direction to go
So I turned up an alley
That life didn't know

As I walked angry masked
At the fight I'd just had
I was raging, jealous
And even quite sad

How a man could betray
Act don't love me no more
All the life, warmth and trust
Packed and went out the door

A man who I thought
Was a million to one
Had gave up our life
For some meaningless fun

And now I was stuck
In depression so true
Was this all I achieved
Out of me loving you

And then suddenly I turned
Heard a noise frantic pose
To my ultimate horror
Stood smack at my nose

Strange man now me captured
Posed threat where I stood
Revolver in hand
Stole my womanhood

As I lay there bare naked
Stripped of all specs of life
Don't know how I should end
With my pills or knife

With my blade to my wrist
Hear my conscious scream
May have took vicious measures
But my soul is supreme

Everything you have lost
Can one day be replaced
Through the power of prayers
And God holy grace

So I mustered up all
Of the strength that I had
Let my soul take me out
Of a life was so bad

Now I count up my blessings
Don't know what life may bring
But am honored to share
Baby girls wedding ring

WILLIE

Willie lives much like a hermit
Down by the railroad tracks
He doesn't bother anyone
Just hangs around this old shack

Sporting authentic hobo shoes
A bedraggled over coat
All the family that he has
Is a tom cat and a goat

In the evening, when the sun goes down
And Willies full on mutton soup
He plays a mean harmonica
Sitting out on his home made stoop

Now don't feel sorry for him
He may have more than me and you
Cause Willie's always smiling
He doesn't worry like we do

SAFE HAVEN

I cannot shake this pain
No matter how I try
Cause everything within my life
Turns out to be a lie

A trusting individual
Would give her last
Feels like the world is drowning her
My GOD she's sinking fast

I don't know what I've done
To make my life a living hell
I'm withering in sorrow
And don't feel very well

I ask the lord to guide me
Need some help along the way
For I feel that I've been cursed somehow
And all my life will pay

I guess that I must use my guards
Protect this thing called love
Until the time I go back home
My safe haven above

CURIOUSITY

The postman came and left a box
That wasn't meant for me
I wonder what is in that box
So filled with mystery

I didn't order anything
So where did it come from
There is no name, just an address
Now isn't that kind of dumb

Curiosity killed the cat
As the saying goes
Will it do the same for me
If I should peek and probe

I'll just set it in the corner
While I go about my chores
I can't concentrate on my house work
Maybe I should go out doors

Ill give it back to the postman
I don't think I want to see
For whatever is inside that box
Might be the end of me

I AM

I have this prized possession
Men constantly try to get
It travels right below me
I cherish and protect

I'm master of the circus
Should hear my lions roar
I walk the highest tight rope
And through the air I soar

I'm wealthiest of richest
My father is the king
And when I enter the palace
Should hear the peasant's sing

I have the purest offer
Of veggies and a lamb
Monogamous of ladies
Provide for all my fam

I am multi-millionaire
Possess the finest jewels
Can give you all you need in life
Plus, luxury and cruise

But out of all the things you give
One thing you never said
I have respect and patience dear
Real love that lies ahead

So my mother is a sister
And I too am a nun
Now when you get the urge to play
Go somewhere else for fun

THE STRANGER

On a cold and dreary winters night
As I huddled round the stove
I could hear the wind a howlin
As it laid the ground with snow

I heard a knock on my front door
And I answered in surprise
There was the most terrifying stranger
With a beard and beady eyes

He stepped inside and looked around
In a most suspicious way
I was wondering what was on his mind
What price was I to pay

He said that he was hungry
And to fix him up a plate
I just wondered what he'd do to me
If I should hesitate

I couldn't think about that now
Oh why was I so dumb
To let this stranger in my house
What was yet to come

I filled the plate the best I could
Of what food I could find
Then I closed my eyes and prayed
Cause I was running out of time

I wondered what he'd do to me
If I should break and run
What kind of weapon would he use
A bat, a knife, a gun

I waited for the end to come
I opened my eyes and he was gone
But left a note for me to read
And this is what it said

I wouldn't ever hurt you
You were so kind you see
But the next time a stranger comes along
He may not be as nice as me

REFLECTION

I looked into the mirror
And couldn't see myself
Instead I saw a woman
With pro-longed declining health

She had these darkened circles
Revolved around her eyes
She looked so worn and tired
Angry, lost and quite despised

And then there was the droopiness
Which covered half her face
It wasn't picture perfect
Just seemed so out of place

I stared a little harder
To see what I could find
A wrinkle past her forehead
Gray hair not formed with time

She had this sullen look
Like all was truly lost
Her dull and gray complexion
Once bright, arrayed with gloss

I stared into the mirror
And thought she looks so sad
That poor and broken woman
A weak and lonely chad

But then it finally hit me
Oh no, this could not be
That worn out dreadful woman
Was no one else but me

I mustered up all energy
And strength that I could find
To heal my broken spirit
A woman once refined

SORRY MISTAKES

You made a mistake when you said I do
And took me for your bride
You made a mistake when you said you're a man
When you're only a boy inside

You made a mistake when you helped me
Give birth to your only son
You made a mistake when you told me
That I was the only one

You made a mistake when you realized
You were a married man
You made a mistake and told me
I wasn't the one in your plans

Blessed these mistakes for showing me
A person I really don't like
But make no mistake when I tell you
You can go and take a hike

DON'T TELL ME

Don't tell me that you love me
Then show me it's not true
Don't want to hear your echoes
But actions loud from you

Don't buy me pretty jewelry
That tarnish at the site
Cause I like stone cut diamonds
That sparkle in the night

Don't flatter me with roses
And charms not mean so much
Your hands are filled with roughness
Not pleasant to the touch

Don't want to hear I'm special
Your only one and all
When you find it for pleasure
To court the girly mall

Don't have the time to listen
To fairytale I do's
Just miss me with the madness
And let the door hit you

YESTERDAY

It seems like only yesterday
I looked upon my child
And saw her playing happily
With her toys and dolls

I liked to shop and buy her clothes
And dress her up real cute
Braid some pig tails in her hair
And watch her scamper down the stairs

But then one day it happened
It seemed like overnight
My little girl grew up on me
And was a lovely sight

She no longer wanted toys or dolls
And pigtails in her hair
But instead she wanted bigger things
A juke box and more hair

I couldn't help but wonder
As I looked upon her face
Will she turn out to become a hood
Or a lady blessed with style and grace

THE MIRROR

I looked into the mirror
Saw self both in and out
Being of GODS creation
Standing strong, erect and stout

I stared at my reflection
Searched myself from head to toe
And thanked the lord that everything
Was in the spot it go

I thought I looked quite beautiful
And wouldn't change a thing
Cause I myself am quite unique
The world's most precious dream

But as they say with beauty
Comes a source from deep within
So I took a closer peak inside
To where it all began

Had thought that all my organs
Was caged where they belonged
But looking much deeper inside
A couple were caged wrong

My brain had slid out to the side
It looked to fall apart
The pieces that were not intact
Had fell upon my heart

I knew my heart felt heavy
From years of wear and tear
But couldn't feel without my brain
Depressed, distraught, despair

Just when I thought I saw the worst
Dear lord, oh GOD behold
The devil came and staked his claim
Tore out my very soul

I fell down on my very knees
Prayed GOD, up high, above
Wrapped me with arms of glory
With inner peace and love

He put my brain back in it's cage
And dusted off my heart
He breathed me life, renewed my soul
Once torn my world apart

Today I face this mirror
With life GOD gave anew
And inner, outer beauty
Courageous, strong and true

I face the mirror everyday
And look both up and down
Inside at GODs creation
A life he changed around

MY MISFORTUNE

Did something ever hurt you
So bad and deep inside
You don't know which direction
To turn or where to hide

Someone drops right out of your life
After years of being there
Your insides are a total wreck
Your hurt and in despair

It's like a dream you cannot touch
No matter how hard you try
You stand there in a state of shock
You cry and wonder why

You think this child was born to me
For me to love and cherish
It didn't cross my mind you see
That someday he would parish

You hear about this happening
To others all the time
And feel awful for them
But say, oh no not mine

And then one day it happens
The impossible you see
It made me a believer
It happened to me

I felt my life was over
For this just couldn't be
That little boy GOD took away
Was a part of me

I felt that I had been betrayed
Or was it something I had done
To be punished so unmercifully
And lose my only son

And now sometimes when I feel sad
And that nobody cares
GOD puts his arms around me
To let me know he's there

He takes away some of the pain
He knows what I can bare
He gives me strength to carry on
He's left three daughters in my care

Now I realize
He wasn't ours alone
He lent him to us for a while
And now he's gone back home

STRANGER

A stranger once approached me
Asked me what I could spare
I didn't have much money
Financially drained, bare

And I had lack of energy
To face another day
My family had disowned me
My life in disarray

But still I gave him only
The little change I had
His eyes were sparkling shiny
His smile was ever glad

He said I want to thank you
Because this meant so much
Your precious, kindred spirit
The way my heart you've touched

He reached into his pocket
And much to my surprise
Gave me a thousand dollars
A blessing to my eyes

DESTRUCTIVE WORLD

The world has gone hay wire
Everything is going on
There's so much crime and violence
Going on from dusk to dawn

It's happening every second
Of each and every day
Never minding all the warnings
That says crime just doesn't pay

The dogs are even turning on you
What happened to man's best friend
Do your think that even they know
The world is coming to an end

Little babies and children
Who can't fight back in their defense
How can anyone abuse them
Does that make any sense

There's still a lot of prejudice
People can't seem to get along
They think the world belongs to them
They've got to know that this is wrong

Our society is made up
Of every race and creed
Only to be taken over
By violence and greed

There's no difference in us really
Except pigmentation of the skin
Cause were all gone be together
When the day of judgement comes again

It's too bad we have to be reminded
That the earth is for everyone
We all were meant to be here
We all share the same bright sun

Folks are killing their own loved ones
Explanations remain unknown
What happened to the meaning of
There's no place like home

LOVELESS

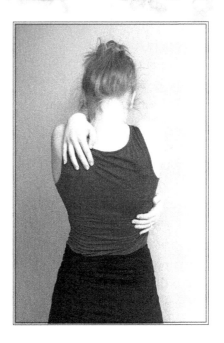

You told me that you loved me
Held what you said as true
You flattered me with roses
And made my world anew

You gave me all the finest
And precious things in life
You said if I behaved myself
One day I'd be your wife

You honored me and sheltered me
Kept me all to yourself
I was your prized possession
Your trophy on the shelf

You said put down your guards now
For I will be your guide
You planned my life, supported me
My only to confide

Aware of what had happened
Felt things were not quite right
You snatched from me my freedom
My world was black as night

You threatened both my future
And dreams had yet to come
You turned my world flip side down up
I've never felt so dumb

But now I've started over
And pledged my life anew
Can't tell me that you love me
Before I love me too

MY SON

It was a cold, late night
Heard a knock at my door
I looked up at the clock
Said ten minutes past four

I put on my clothes
And went down to see
Who could be calling
At this hour for me

I opened the door
Two cops dressed in blue
Told me we've come
With a message for you

They told me, my son
Had been shot, and he's dead
Someone had put a bullet
In his back and his head

I said no way
This just couldn't be
My son will be in soon
He'll be right here with me

But as the night cleared
And dawn was in sight
My son still wasn't home
Did that happen last night

I found out it was true
And my heart sank so low
How could anyone survive
Such a terrible blow

That was my boy
My flesh, my seed
How could someone erase
A child of my need

I wonder if they thought
About what they had done
Like a thief in the night
They had shot down my son

I hope everytime
That a bullet rings out
They'll think of that night
When they took my son out

The pain in my heart
Just would not leave
So I got on my knees
And asked the lord please

Help me with this
Lift this burden from me
I can't do it alone
I need your help please

MY BEAUTIFUL DAUGHTERS

I have two special daughters
Was sent from up above
I spoil them and shower them
With mother's special love

Give each and everyday to them
Of everything I have
Remove all their bumps for them
To make a smoother path

I listen to their problems
And feel it in my heart
Lead them in the right direction
From the very start

I teach them about values
And morals in their life
Until their soul mate comes along
And makes them his wife

Thank GOD he gave them to me
Placed them in my care
I doctor all their bruises
Put corn rolls in their hair

I watch them each and everyday
As a woman comes
I'd give my very breath to them
Exhale out from my lungs

I feel their ups and downs with them
Both pain and happiness
There's nothing like the bond we share
Me and my two princess

DAD

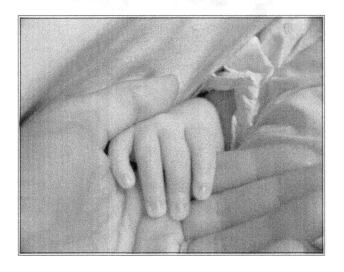

Here's a few lines to let you know
Though words cannot express
The way we feel about you dad
With love and tenderness

You always were so thoughtful
In helping everyone
You never thought about yourself
Until your work was done

If they were giving trophies
For ones we love so dear
Your name would be the first in line
For father of the year

THE ULTIMATE PROPOSAL

I woke up bright and early
First peak of the morn
My heart was racing panthers
For love me to adorn

My hands were sticky sweaty
For what was yet to come
Uncertain of the moment
Was dazed and feeling numb

My hair was quite disheveled
My face in disarray
Unbeknownst what would hit me
For strength dear lord I pray

And then I popped the question
As I fell down on one knee
Dear precious special lady
Will I marry me?

My face turned bright as lightning
My smile wide as the sea
Had waited for this moment
For all eternity

For I'll never forsake thee
Will cherish me at best
Give nothing less commitment
Till my hearts laid to rest

I'll honor and protect me
And always put me first
And never will I leave me
Through healthy times and worst

For there's no other person
With whom I'd like to be
No one could even measure
The bride GOD gave in me

Oh yes I'd take thee honor
And soon to be my wife
There's no other more deserving
Of my love and all my life

I'll always keep my promise
And never treat me bad
To honor and protect me
Through good times and through bad

HEAVENLY FATHER

Almighty father up above
You created this earth with peace and love
You made the sun to light our day
And give us heat from golden rays

You made the trees to bare us fruit
And then some extra to give us shade
You put the clouds high in the sky
And from them our rain is made

To water the plants that give us food
And fill the lakes to house our fish
To give us water that we may drink
And nourish our brains from which we think

You made the animals the birds that fly
The twinkling stars up in the sky
You planted flowers all over the land
But best of all you created man

VULNERABLE

I used to sit and think about
The way our life could be
Articulated every move
Fulfilled my fantasy

I put you on this pedestal
For what I hoped to come
And labeled instantaneously
My perfect number one

Imagined situations
That only true love brings
And then I even went so far
And tried on wedding rings

You see I gave more credit
Then you should have had
And now I see true colors
I'm angry, hurt and sad

I only focused on you
Let expectations soar
That's when you took for granted
Ripped through my heart you tore

I should have never let you in
Was vulnerable you see
A fast fix for a broken heart
That you played viciously

GROWING OLD

I sit here contemplating
Of things that's on my mind
And wonder what life's all about
And why is it so blind

I think about the teenagers
And the ones that's soon to be
I wonder what goes through their minds
I wonder what they see

They seem to grow up faster
Then they did when I was young
And oh, they just know everything
From the kids they hang among

They don't have time to listen
To a word of good advice
When you're only trying to teach them
About the facts of life

But I know as they grow up
They'll think back to this day
They'll sit and contemplate themselves
And wonder what to say

To their children as they grow up
They'll say was I like that?
No wonder that my elders
Tried to tell me where it's at

HEAVEN BOUND

I saw my friend the other day
And asked how she was doing
She said her life was quite corrupt
And in a state of ruin

I didn't hesitate one bit
To ask her what she meant
She said her boy was heaven bound
Recently GOD sent

I asked her what had happened
On that awful dreadful day
She told me that a bullet
Had took her son away

She didn't know the reason
Why he called her son that night
I told her that he was okay
Cause GOD showed him the light

She said things hadn't been the same
Since her son disappeared
She sweats, she shakes, can't sleep at night
Her days are sort of weird

I asked if she could listen
To a word of good advice
Assured her that her pain inside
With GODS help would suffice

One day we'll find our meeting grounds
With loved ones from our past
Till then our fondest memories
Forever on will last

A DREAM

A dream is but a fantasy
Realistically inclined
It stretches the imagination
And intrudes upon your mind

It's images of what's within
Your inner utmost soul
It's fantasy of reruns
With no future or no goal

Some are so ridiculous
Which means your minds a mess
Some are filled with sorrow
And some with happiness

When you lay down and close your eyes
You drift way out to sea
You can't decipher which it is
A play or reality

Much later when you awaken
You may be glad or sad
It depends upon the dream you see
Like was it good or bad

PERCEPTIONS

I'm struggling with these feelings
So deep inside my soul
I tell them life is happy
They tell me life is cold

I tell them with pure dedication
All things can be achieved
They tell me that's all hope and dreams
And fantasies believed

I tell them that I'll focus
And love will come my way
They tell me that I'm stupid
And with heartbreak I will pay

I tell them I'm deserving
Of nothing but the best
They tell me not to kid myself
A failure to life's test

I tell them that I'm brilliant
Intelligent of kind
They tell me no one see's me
And each day I'm slowly dying

I ask if they could help me
To change the way I feel
They tell me that it's up to me
Perceptions at the wheel

In life we get to make the choice
Of how we want to feel
The good, the bad the happiness
The healthy life and ill

It all depends upon the way
We chose to look at things
Depressed slaves of the madness
Or the merry life or queens

A PLEA FOR HELP

It's a sad situation
When you're down on your luck
With no one to help you
They just pass the buck

Telling you the things
That you should have done
To keep your life perfect
And be number one

Everybody makes mistakes
No one is exempt
They say they're going to help you
But they make no attempt

One day they'll need help too
And nobody will care
They'll look for someone
And nobody's there

One thing I need to stress in life
Do others as they should do you
You never know who you may have to call
When you're struggling in life to get through

REBORN

If I could have one wish in life
You know what it would be
To live stress free, true happiness
For all eternity

I'd first start to eliminate
Things tugging at my heart
They have the greatest impact
They leave me torn apart

And then I'd go and tackle
The things that stress my brain
The worries, insecurities
In which no hope remains

And after that's accomplished
I'd go and cleanse my soul
Release all the impurities
My body tried to hold

Then I could take thee honor
To begin my life again
Vibrant, refreshed, free spirit
Like when life first began

OUR LOST BOYS

Everything is changed today
From what it used to be
There's so much violence in the streets
It's just not the same you see

You're scared to let your children
Go outside to play
Anything could happen
To one of them some day

Every block is territorial
Don't even cross that line
Cause what could happen to you
May not be so kind

Every day when I awake
I wonder in my head
How many boys were shot last night
How many boys are dead

All our young men are leaving
Being wiped out one by one
Never imagining this is their time
To be taken out by someone's gun

Maybe things will change some day
Only time will tell
But at this rate well lose them all
They'll be dead or locked in jail

BEST FRIEND

I've always been your best friend
I your Bonnie, you my Clyde
We'd sit and talk for hours
Share dreams, laugh and confide

We never stopped one moment
A penny for your thoughts
That warmth and comfort feeling
Every day we sought

I never had felt lonely
Not with your presence near
I'd lay my head upon your chest
You'd rub and stroke my hair

We'd ride off into the sunset
And dream of years to come
A life we built on happiness
Was soon to be as one

You protected me and kept me close
I never felt a threat
And all the needs and wants I had
Superior you met

I'd never felt so confident
Knew that you'd always care
There's nothing like the life we lived
Or the bond we shared

And on that awesome, special day
You took me in your life
My dreams and prayers answered
I now pronounce your wife

I'll never disappoint you
Always be by your side
You'll always be my best friend
I your Bonnie, you my Clyde

STRONG BLACK WOMAN

I'm a strong black woman
I can do most anything
My mind is prepared
For whatever life brings

I don't possess a degree
Just mental telepathy
If you want to know something
Just come and ask me

I'm a strong black woman
I can cook and clean
And at the same time
Be every man's dream

There are so many things
That I can do
Physically, mentally
And spiritually too

I don't need anyone
To tell me who I am
Just come get this knowledge
And life could be glam

PURPOSE IN LIFE

You asked what was your purpose
Why you were put on earth
Mistreated and neglected
Abused beyond your worth

Fatigued and drained of energy
Bruised well from in your past
No strength to fight another day
Want rest, to lay at last

Your blinded by unpleasantness
And now you've lost all hope
You tried to cure you pain inside
With alcohol and dope

Your man who's now your enemy
You're forced to take to court
Refuse to help raise his own kids
So you seek child support

And if this isn't quite enough
He beats you everyday
You're worried, frightened, all alone
Think justice doesn't pay

Your voice just keeps on haunting me
I feel your pain quite deep
You're more deserving than you feel
My heart for you does weep

Your purpose is the same in life
As everyone of us
GOD made us all of equal beings
To rule the earth in just

You have to use the strength he gives
Your life you need to cherish
You're allowing men to take your soul
This way all dreams will parish

Don't put anyone before the lord
Your purpose true, less fear
And thank him each and every day
On earth he put you here

For if he had no purpose
On earth you'd not remain
Stop taking life for granted
And praise his holy name

NATURE

The day is light
The sun is bright
I look outside
With pure delight

The flowers are so beautiful
I can't believe my eyes
The clouds are forming pictures
In our big beautiful blue sky

Hence let this day last forever
And not to give in
To rain, cold and darkness
And oh, that awful wind

The grass evergreen
With daises delight
And the suns brightest sunbeams
Blanket the sky

We are truly quite blessed
What a wonderful life
Giving praise of our nations
Respect to our rites

VAMPIRE

The man I chose to marry
Is a vampire you see
He had the sharpest teeth of all
He put his fangs in me

He ripped into my life one day
And turned my world around
I thought I had a lover
A partner true and sound

He told me all beautiful things
The things I'd love to hear
Then turned me to the other side
To whisper in my ear

He said he'd always love me
Seduced me from the start
I didn't know deep down inside
He'd tear my world apart

He had the greatest way
Of professing his love for me
Inside his world I'd want to live
For all eternity

No sooner as I gave my hand
Turned to thee other side
The demons he had locked away
Could not, no longer hide

Drained me of all my energy
As he sucked away my blood
And if this wasn't quite enough
My heart he chose to flood

I found myself now flying
Through the contours of the night
A road so bumpy lay ahead
In my future plight

I don't know where I'm headed
Cross this long, cold, chilling flight
But dear GOD please save me from terrain
And lead me back to light

A PICTURE OF SELF WORTH

What kind of person am I?
Always pushing others away
I guess I talk to much at times
And don't know what to say

If only I would learn to be quiet
And just don't say a word
Keep my lips closed tightly
So my voice will not be heard

People think that I'm illiterate
And don't know what to say
Instead of talking to me
They just turn and walk away

I just asked for simple things
A little errand now and then
And Lord knows I wasn't thinking
That this could really be a sin

I can't even have a decent conversation
On the phone with so called friends
You have to guard each word you say
Or your friendships coming to an end

It takes a lot of will power
To keep my mouth closed tight
But as long as I keep working on it
Everything will be alright

DEAR LORD

I ask you lord to guide me
Give me strength throughout my day
To make it through the pitfalls
That I pass along the way

To lift my inner spirits
Shine your light onto my heart
Release my sins and turmoil
From my soul, it torn apart

Give me the will and confidence
I will need throughout my plight
And never leave my side, dear Lord
Please guide me day and night

When things seem much too hard for me
Things I can't seem to bare
Please let me feel your presence near
Remove hurt and despair

I've been through many things in life
Don't quite know what to do
So now I'm putting down my guards
And all my faith in you

I trust you lord, I'll follow you
From this day and through all
Cause I know you'll be right here for me
And never let me fall

I'll pray to you in heaven
Every day I'll speak your name
And whatever life shall throw my way
My faith in you remains

MISTREATED

You were born in this day and age
To be loved and cared for
With someone to look up to
Someone you'd adore

But instead you were mistreated
And much underfed
The people who's supposed to protect you
Are the parents you've come to dread

Remember the day
You had that bump on your head
When your mommy got drunk
And kicked you out of the bed

You hid in the closet
Till day light came
Then you had to come out
Cause they kept calling your name

You were kept out of school
Till the bruise went away
And so no one would notice
What happened that day

Your stomach would hurt
And your head would thrive
You just had enough food
To keep you alive

They would send you to school
With a bruise here and there
You tried to tell them what happened
But nobody cared

When it was time to go home
Your smile left your face
Cause you had to go back
To that dreadful place

Maybe my guardian angel will come
And save me from hurt and despair
She'll take me away, to a better place
Cause no one here seems to care

MISTAKES

I gave my very heart away
Time and time again
I didn't think about the risk
Importance of true friends

Was told all I wanted to hear
I would be treated best
Put all of my defenses down
Too fast our time progressed

Was showered with attention
And flattered the utmost
And when you said I'm quite the gem
On you I bragged and boast

Said you would be here for me
Would never leave my side
I thought I'd found my rock indeed
My troubles to confide

And then that magic moment
I laid upon your bed
I felt such pleasure deep within
All doubts were pronounced dead

No sooner than this happened
You turned thee other cheek
Our conversations shortened
Companionship to seek

I barely got a call from you
My troubles? Ceased to care
And when I needed you the most
You never, wasn't there

It's funny how the two of us
Chose to take it deep
And now you have the nerves to treat
Me worthless and cheap

You've never done much growing
Your offerings slim to none
The only machoness you feel
Is your bb gun

GLOOM

I'm losing all reality
My hope is fading fast
My stomachs feeling queasy
My migraines on full blast

I'm dying in the inside
The pressures on my soul
I'm drained of all my energy
My bodies turning old

The brightest colors seem to me
So dim, much less of gloss
I feel so all alone sometimes
Like all connections lost

I'm wanting, reaching, yelling
Someone in me to hold
The longing, louder that I yell
The pain becomes ten-fold

My mind is turning twisted
Is what's supposed to be?
Thought hell would be on judgment day
Not here on earth with me

FACEBOOK DEMONS

A thousand eyes are watching
As you step onto the stage
To see the biggest failure
And the life which they engaged

They feed onto your stories
Waiting for the ones you flawed
And dig their claws deep in your soul
Your heart, your spirit mawed

Could care less about your problems
Or your worries out their sight
To joke about your issues
With sheer, utter delight

I found myself so saddened
Not a friend for me to call
To console me past my troubled days
And longest, darkest hauls

But what is most disturbing
How they change one's life for death
With no regards for family
Loved ones behind they've left

Some people broadcast suicides
As they step onto the stage
And pull the trigger viciously
As millions watch engaged

And the prejudices come out
As the site of them trans heed
To cast upon the innocence
With hateful eyes and greed

And what about the ones who claim
They love you, you're the test
To settle scores from long ago
And stroke their egos best

I guess it builds some's confidence
Opens doors for them to cheat
Cause their physical vitalities
Were always at defeat

Whenever I shall settle down
In life, whole and complete
The Facebook demons will summize
Cause I'll just press delete

MY HEALTH

Everyday my body hurts
While I sit silently in pain
Yet I suffer from insomnia
Will I ever sleep again?

I'm taking medicine for my nerves
I hope the pain will go away
And my body will recover
And be normal again someday

They say I need to walk
Thirty minutes in each day
I don't know how I'm gonna do it
But I have to find a way

They kicked me out of therapy
Said I wasn't there enough
So I'll have to find another way
To make my body tough

CARELESS

I went out on a windy
Saturday night
With my tight fitted dress
My pumps and my tights

Looked quite captivating
As I walked in the club
All the eyes were on me
Which gave proof that I was

I sat with my girlfriends
My cousins, we all
Laughed, joked
Yes we had a ball

As the music got louder
I got up on my feet
And I moved with perfection
Oh yes! I looked sweet

Then I don't know what happened
Towards middle past night
Girls approached by my table
And started a fight

Now we all know the truth
There's no fist fights no more
One minute, two, three past
Best friends on the floor

Was shot at close angle
Then left there to die
I cuddled, cried, screamed
Lord, why Trina, not I?

Now what would I tell
Trina's parents and kin
And how would I live now
Without my best friend

The night could have been different
Not deadly I figure
If they had thought with their brains
And their hands off the trigger

OLD AGE

I want something from the store
Every now and then
But maybe I should shut my mouth
And never ask again

You'd think that since I don't drive
They'd ask me when they go
Is there something that you need today
If yes just tell me so

I don't mean to be a bother
Really don't, I mean no harm
I need to think like old folks do
And just not give a darn

You need to do things for yourself
And make the best of it
Don't let small things get you down
You're not the one to quit

HAIR DAYS

I remember the day
Were you aware?
How it hurt
When you combed my hair

I wanted to scream
And cry for help
But the comb kept ripping
Cross my scalp

Oh, how awful
To be born this way
And have my hair
Combed everyday

There is nothing
I can do
To plead my case
And convince you

How bad it hurt
When you combed my hair
But there's just so much
My head could bare

I can't wait
Till my head is grown
And can strike out
On its own

Without the torture
And the scare
I can do my
Very own hair

Printed in the United States
By Bookmasters